Restore

REBUILDING YOUR RELATIONSHIP WITH GOD

By: Troyal Tillman

Restore
Rebuilding Your Relationship with God
By Troyal Tillman

Printed in the United States of America
Royalty Publishing, 2022
ISBN **978-1-7369914-5-9**
Royalty Publishing, LLC
Ponchatoula, La

The purpose of this book is to help you build a stronger relationship with God whether you are a believer or non-believer. Jesus Christ died so that we would be forgiven for our sins. There is no sin too great that Jesus can't cover, but you must believe, repent, and you must obey. God only wants your commitment if you are willing to give it to him. Your commitment doesn't only guarantee you a greater covering, but it guarantee's you everlasting life. This book will go over foundational necessities to ensure that you as a reader can evaluate your heart, mind, and your life and be assured in your commitment to Christ. You will also be able to go over biblical testimonies that you will be able to learn and be strengthen from. I personally want to thank you for believing in the work of God through this written book and I pray that God will open your eyes to see him in ways you have never seen him. I also pray that every word will become life for you, so that you will experience God's word as a reality,

 in the name of Jesus Christ,

Amen.

-*Troyal Tillman*

Table of Contents

Introduction

Have you ever been in a close relationship with someone and eventually the relationship loses connection? When distance starts to take place, you notice you do not talk as much as you did and do things like you use too and you can't seem to point out the reason your relationship is dissolving or has dissolved. It is easy to assume you've grown apart because your life and their life has gone in different directions, right. Or have you experienced losing a relationship because of offense and as a result of the offense, you're hurt so you decide to step away, but time doesn't heal, it only caused more distance? Or what about this, have you ever spoken about a person and had either positive or negative feelings about the individual and never actually established a relationship, so your information was based off someone else's opinion or experience?

Relationships usually do not exist because one has not taken the opportunity to get to know the other party or either lose connection because commitment decreases. Commitment to keep connecting through love and communication. When the love fades and offense or selfishness increases and communication decreases, connection is lost.

But imagine losing connection with someone that you cannot live without or feeling like you know there is something you are missing, but you can't put your finger on it. What do you do? You come to the conclusion that it's time to discover what you're missing or restore your broken relationship by any means necessary, you make the decision to re- establish the relationship, but you change the things that causes the relationship to fail.

You are reading this book because somewhere down the line you have experienced feeling the void, desiring a deeper relationship, or you have lost your connection with God and you feel like you cannot see him, hear him, or his promises spoken over your life are not a reality. And you want to know what is wrong, so instead of giving up completely, you desire a relationship that is stronger and better than the relationship you once knew. You have come to the conclusion that your relationship with God is one you can not live without, so you've decided to restore your relationship.

In this book you will do a layering of study through the word that will establish the Godly foundation that results in a successful relationship with God. You will be able to sit and evaluate your character and learn about who God is and who he is to you. You will be able to establish trust and better communication (prayer) with God. And you will be able to establish a true father & child relationship as well as a friendship with God. Your love for him will surely increase.

Before you begin your study, Pray this prayer:

Father, I want to know you and I want to experience you and all your realness in my daily life. I am so sorry that I've gone this far without holding your hand as I should've. Father, open and increase my understanding as I learn about who you are and erase every lie and remove every spirit and distraction that has brought a wedge between you and I. Father, I desire to change and I ask that you reveal yourself to me, so that I can have a better and stronger relationship with you.

In the name of Jesus Christ

, Amen.

Sent Savior

"My little children, these things write I unto you, that ye sin not. And if any man sin, we have an advocate with the Father, Jesus Christ the righteous."

1 John 2:1

The Fall

Have you ever had the falling dream? Imagine yourself falling and falling and falling and feeling all the fear and the intensity growing as fear increases because you know that death is near and then suddenly you find yourself swept away out of danger and placed on solid ground. Sounds like a movie right, but this is real life for every person and Jesus Christ is the savior that comes in and rescues each and every one of us from this great fall.

Now you may be the individual that feels like everything is going wrong no matter how hard you try and you can't seem to catch a break therefore you feel the fall or you may be the person that says, my life is great, I may have a few hiccups but I'm not falling, but one's falling is not determined by the things obtained but the sins committed and sin separates anyone from God. And where there is separation there you will find a non-existent or a failing relationship.

Sins by whom you ask? By our first father and mother, by past generations, and by you.

The first sin happened in the Garden of Eden when God gave the commandment to Adam to never eat of the fruit from the tree of knowledge of good and evil. Genesis 2:15-17, *"And the LORD God took the man, and put him into the garden of Eden to dress it and to keep it.*

(16)And the LORD God commanded the man, saying, Of every tree of the garden thou mayest freely eat: (17) But of tree of the knowledge of good and evil, thou shalt not eat of it: for in the day that thou eatest thereof thou shalt surely die." Later in Genesis 3, God's commandment was not obeyed due to temptation. *"Now the serpent was more subtil than any beast of the field which the LORD God had made. And he said unto the woman, Yea, hath God said, Ye shall not eat of every tree of the garden?(2)And the woman said unto the serpent, We may eat*

of the fruit of the trees of the garden:(3)But of the fruit of the tree which is in the midst of the garden, God hath said, Ye shall not eat of it, neither shall ye touch it, lest ye die.(4)And the serpent said unto the woman, Ye shall not surely die:(5)For God doth know that in the day ye eat thereof, then your eyes shall be opened, and ye shall be as gods, knowing good and evil.(6)And when the woman saw that the tree was good for food, and that it was pleasant to the eyes, and a tree to be desired to make one wise, she took of the fruit thereof, and did eat, and gave also unto her husband with her; and he did eat. (7) And the eyes of them both were opened, and they knew that they were naked;", this is Genesis 3:1-7.

I want you to take notice that they had a good life, which is translated to a perfect life, a holy life, fully provided for and protected, until sin came in. This disobedience resulted in sin being brought into the world causing the first and great fall of humankind. There are so many questions an individual would have, and some would say why would the tree even be there, but no one truly knows that answer, but God himself. But what we do know is that through this example we observe God's desire to establish good without evil, mankind's free will, and God's relationship was one that was with choice by man and to be solely dependent on him being their source. In addition, take note there were two significant trees in the garden (Scripture Ref. Genesis 2:9). The other being the tree of life, and this tree was not forbidden of and results of eating from it would have been eternal life. However, the choice of eating from the forbidden tree cancelled out the option of then eating from the tree of life along with many other things. "And the LORD God said, Behold, the man is become as one of us, to know good and evil: and now, lest he put forth his hand, and take also of the tree of life, and eat, and live for ever:(23)Therefore the LORD God sent him forth from the garden of Eden, to till the ground from whence he was taken. (24)So he drove out the man; and he placed at the east of the garden of Eden Cherubims, and a flaming sword which turned every way, to keep the way of the tree of life" Genesis 3:22-24

As you read, Genesis 3 breaks down this major occurrence that happened that disrupted the very good life and good of all existence God planned for humankind and it started with the first man, Adam and Woman, known as Eve. Now the consequence of their disobedience was death and sin, amongst many other things, which was brought on by themselves in addition, God did punish them. "And the LORD God said unto the serpent, Because thou hast done this, thou *art* cursed above all cattle, and above every beast of the field; upon thy belly shalt thou go, and dust shalt thou eat all the days of thy life:(15)And I will put enmity between thee and the woman, and between thy seed and her seed; it shall bruise thy head, and thou shalt bruise his heel.(16)Unto the woman he said, I will greatly multiply thy sorrow and thy conception; in sorrow thou shalt bring forth children; and thy desire *shall be* to thy husband, and he shall rule over thee.(17)And unto Adam he said, Because thou hast hearkened unto the voice of thy wife, and hast eaten of the tree, of which I commanded thee, saying, Thou shalt not eat of it: cursed *is* the ground for thy sake; in sorrow shalt thou eat *of* it all the days of thy life;(18)Thorns also and thistles shall it bring forth to thee; and thou shalt eat the herb of the field;(19)In the sweat of thy face shalt thou eat bread, till thou return unto the ground; for out of it wast thou taken: for dust thou art, and unto dust shalt thou return." Genesis 3:14-19. As you just read, the serpent, Eve, and Adam all were punished with a curse, but even in that

God had a plan in store that would restore the plan of the good eternal life he had from the beginning. There was not any man that could be found without blame that God can use to restore his relationship and purpose back with humankind. The generations of people continued to disobey God. Isaiah 58:12 lets us in on a message Isaiah had for God's people, "And they that shall be of thee shall build the old waste places: thou shalt raise up the foundations of many generations; and thou shalt be called, the repairer of the breach, the restorer of paths to dwell in." which gives insight on the people needing to remove the generational ruins and restore and re-establish the true foundation of God. This is a scripture from which we must learn. To not continue in the wicked foundations that has been passed down from generation to generations, which can be iniquity. There must be a cancellation of all bad habits, characteristics, and traditions. Just because you are accustomed and comfortable to it does not mean it is right. There is one law that is proven to be just and righteous. The law of God, which is all righteous and pure. It cannot lead you down the wrong path.

The moment you begin to question God's righteousness or even get above yourself and believe all that you are and have been because of self is an open opportunity for Satan to use as a tactic to cause you to fall. Did you know that Satan fell as well and now his purpose is to destroy you, He is against humankind and especially those who surrender to God. The bible tells us in John 10:10, "The thief cometh not, but for to steal, and to kill, and to destroy." And so, you are not fooled to who Satan is and his tactics, here's what the word of God gives us insight in. Ezekiel 28: 13-19 informs us about Satan's fall, "Thou hast been in Eden the garden of God; every precious stone *was* thy covering, the sardius, topaz, and the diamond, the beryl, the onyx, and the jasper, the sapphire, the emerald, and the carbuncle, and gold: the workmanship of thy tabrets and of thy pipes was prepared in thee in the day that thou wast created.(14) Thou *art* the anointed cherub that covereth; and I have set thee *so*: thou wast upon the holy mountain of God; thou hast walked up and down in the midst of the stones of fire.(15) Thou *wast* perfect in thy ways from the day that thou wast created, till iniquity was found in thee.(16) By the multitude of thy merchandise they have filled the midst of thee with violence, and thou hast sinned: therefore I will cast thee as profane out of the mountain of God: and I will destroy thee, O covering cherub, from the midst of the stones of fire.(17) Thine heart was lifted up because of thy beauty, thou hast corrupted thy wisdom by reason of thy brightness: I will cast thee to the ground, I will lay thee before kings, that they may behold thee.(18) Thou hast defiled thy sanctuaries by the multitude of thine iniquities, by the iniquity of thy traffick; therefore will I bring forth a fire from the midst of thee, it shall devour thee, and

I will bring thee to ashes upon the earth in the sight of all them that behold thee.(19)All they that know thee among the people shall be astonished at thee: thou shalt be a terror, and never shalt thou be any more."

You see he fell because of self-pride. He became so prideful based off his beauty, his position, and desired honor and glory for himself which can only belong to God, because God was his creator. There was a war in heaven when Satan tried to take God's place. *"And there was war in heaven: Michael and his angels fought against the dragon; and the dragon fought and his angels,(8) And prevailed not; neither was their place found any more in heaven.(9) And the great dragon was cast out, that old serpent, called the Devil, and Satan,* which deceiveth the whole world: he was cast out into the earth, and his angels were cast out with him.(10) And I heard a loud voice saying in heaven, Now is come salvation, and strength, and the kingdom of our God, and the power of his Christ: for the accuser of our brethren is cast down, which accused them before our God day and night.(11)And they overcame him by the blood of the Lamb, and by the word of their testimony; and they loved not their lives unto the death.(12)Therefore rejoice, ye heavens, and ye that dwelt in them. Woe to the inhabiters of the earth and of the sea! For the devilis come down unto you,having great wrath, because he knoweth that he hath but a short time.", Revelations 12:7-12. Satan is never going to be on your side as the word says he is the accuser of the brethren. Think about an accuser's purpose, the purpose is to present claims that someone has done something wrong. So, he wants you to do wrong which is why he comes to tempt you to do wrong so then he can in return accuse you. Presenting you sinful instead of blameless. Remember, he cannot make you do anything, unless you give him access. Consider what happened with Eve in the garden, he came in the form of a serpent, which was created by God, so he deceived her with what God created. He then proceeded to ask a question with God's word, which opened the door for Eve doubt what she was told. That changed her perception of the tree. Satan will never stop attacking the people in this world, which is why it is important to discern him and know his character, so that you will not be so easily deceived.

In Luke 4:1-13, you can find how Satan tried to tempt Jesus and through this test of temptation, Jesus shows us how to overcome Satan when he comes to tempt and deceive, *"And Jesus being full of the Holy Ghost returned from Jordan, and was led by the Spirit into the wilderness,(2) Being forty days tempted of the devil. And in those days he did eat nothing: and when they were ended, he afterward hungered. (3)And the devil said unto him, If thou be the Son of God, command this stone that it be made bread. (4) And Jesus answered him, saying, It is written, That man shall not live by bread alone, but by every word of God. (5) And the devil, taking him up into an high mountain, shewed unto him all the kingdoms of the world in a moment of time.(6) And the devil said unto him, All this power will I give thee, and the glory of them: for that is delivered unto me; and to whomsoever I will I give it. (7) If thou therefore wilt worship me, all shall be thine. (8) And Jesus answered and said unto him, Get thee behind me, Satan: for it is written, Thou shalt worship the Lord thy God, and him only shalt thou serve. (9) And he brought him to Jerusalem, and set him on a pinnacle of the temple, and said unto him, If thou be the Son of God, cast thyself down from hence: (10) For it is written, He shall give his angels charge over thee, to keep thee: (11) And in their hands they shall bear thee up, lest at any time thou dash thy foot against a stone. (12) And Jesus answering said unto him, It is* said, Thou shalt not tempt the Lord thy God.(13)And when the devil had ended all the temptation, he departed from him for a season." You learned through the example of Jesus' test to overcome temptation with the word of God. He tempts with many vices but here we learn he tempts by trying to make us be self-dependent, to operate without God, He tempts with worldly positions and possessions, he also tries to get us off track by making us feel like God must prove himself to us, so he will try to make you test God. He has many tactics but they only way he can gain victory and make a person fall is if the person entertains him and give him access to their mind. The moment you open your mind to see things Satan's way you open yourself up to be a servant to him and he will use you to tear you down more, draw you away from God, and he will also use you to tear down others and become a stumbling block in their way. It is important that you stay in the word so when he comes you will have God's word as a weapon, because Satan must bow down to God's word, not yours, God's word. Satan has no respect and will come after all of God's creations and the only way he can be rebuked is by the Lord himself. Observe in Jude chapter 1 verses nine *how Michael, the archangel withstands Satan. "Yet Michael the archangel, when contending with the devil he disputed about the body of Moses, durst not bring against him a railing accusation, but said, The Lord rebuke thee."* Look how this mighty angel of God handled Satan, he knew the power in God, therefore he simply said, "The Lord rebuke you!" This is important that you know how to handle Satan when he comes, because he is not afraid of you, he only responds to the word of God and God alone. God has a power that cancels every attack and plan of the enemy. God's word is your weapon. You cannot fail with him! Imagine seeing a little lion cub roaring at a beast but the beast that was once ready to pounce at some point runs in fear, not because of the roar of the little lion but because of the roar of the might lion that stood behind the little lion cub. You are that cub, you have authority but the beast that is out to destroy you will only run at the roar of the might lion, the lord. It is not wise to believe that you can make it on your own, you need God.

Remember to follow Jesus, he had victory when he responded with the word of God. God wants to be included in your every move, not to control you but to cover you, you learned from the fall of Satan that pride often comes from the deceptions of self-sufficiency. But because you are not your own you will never be self-sufficient, the truth is you can not maintain without God, for the very breath of life you have, comes from him. The functionality of your body is not dependent on your words, but its in God's hands, you only have the authority ability to maintain what he has given you. Be wise, make the right choice, turn from your selfish ways, surrender your mind and allow God to be Lord over your life every day.

Scripture(s) For Encouragement

"For all have sinned, and come short of the glory of God."
Romans 3:23

"Forasmuch as ye know that ye were not redeemed with corruptible things, as silver and gold, from your vain conversations received by tradition from your fathers." 1 Peter 1:18

"But we are all as an unclean thing, and all our righteousness are as filthy rags; and all we do fade as a leaf; and our iniquities, like the wind, have taken us away." Isaiah 64:6

"Therefore to him that knoweth to do good, and doeth it not, to him it is sin." James 4:17

"But your iniquities have separated between you and your God, and your sins have hid his face from you, that he will not hear." Isaiah 59:2

"Now the works of the flesh are manifest, which are these; Adultery, fornication, uncleanness, lasciviousness, idolatry, witchcraft, hatred, variance, emulations, wrath, strife, seditions, heresies, envyings, murders, drunkenness, revellings, and such like of the which I tell you before, as I have also told you in time past, that

they which do such things shall not inherit the kingdom of God."
Galatians 5:19-21

"If we say that we have no sin, we deceive ourselves, and the truth is not in us.(9) If we confess our sins, he is faithful and just to forgive us our sins, and to cleanse us from all unrighteousness.(10) If we say that we have not sinned, we make him a liar, and his word is not in us."

1 John 8-10

"Mortify therefore your members which are upon the earth; fornication, uncleanness, inordinate affection, evil concupiscence, and

covetousness, which is idolatry:(6) For which things' sake the wrath of God cometh on the children of disobedience:"

Colossians 3:5-6

"Therefore to him that knoweth to do good, and doeth it not, to him it is sin."

James 4:17

What then? shall we sin, because we are not under the law, but under grace? God forbid."

Romans 6:15

"Whosoever committeth sin transgresseth also the law: for sin is the transgression of the law". 1 John 3:4

"For all have sinned, and come short of he glory of God." Romans 3:23

"He that walketh uprightly surely: But he that perverteth his ways shall be known." Proverbs 10:9

Here Comes the Savior

"For God so loved the world, that he gave his only begotten Son, that whosoever believeth in him should not perish, but have everlasting life." John 3:16

(Do a in depth Study of the death of Jesus, it can be found in Matthew Ch.26-Ch.28, Mark Ch.14-Ch. 16, Luke Ch.22- Ch.24, John Ch.17 –Ch.20)

Jesus' death had the purpose to save the world. His death was very tragic, and no man has had to face such a horrible death being innocent but Jesus. In all the miracles and profound lessons Jesus gave, he still had what we call today, HATERS. They were the religious group, the

Pharisees. In addition, he was betrayed by one of his very own disciples named, Judas. Judas went to the priest and asked them what they would give him if he delivered Jesus to them and looked for an opportunity to do it, for in return he received money. One night while in the garden Jesus and his disciples were approached and it was with a kiss Judas identified Jesus for the arrest of Jesus. They then took Jesus to the high priest where they falsely accused him and declared him guilty of death and begin to spit in his face and strike him repeatedly and some hitting him so hard it injured him. By morning, they brought him to the governor, Pontas Pilate who questioned him and presented the option to the multitude, elders, and chief priest to free Jesus or

Barabbas, who was a murderer. They chose Barabbas and repeatedly shouted, "Crucify him." Jesus was then brought to the common hall where soldiers mocked him, stripped him, spit on him, and struck him in his head. These are the moments that happened before his death. Here you will read the word further that will inform you about his crucifixion.

Luke 23:26-49, *"And as they led him away, they laid hold upon one Simon, a Cyrenian, coming out of the country, and on him they laid the cross, that he might bear* it *after Jesus.(27)And there followed him a great company of people, and of women, which also bewailed and lamented him.(28)But Jesus turning unto them said, Daughters of Jerusalem, weep not for me, but weep for yourselves, and for your* children.(29)For, behold, the days are coming, in the which they shall say, Blessed are the barren, and the wombs that never bare, and the paps which never gave suck.(30)Then shall they begin to say to the mountains, Fall on us; and to the hills, Cover us.(31)For if they do these things in a green tree, what shall be done in the dry?(32)And there were also two other, malefactors, led with him to be put to death.(33)And when they were come to the place, which is called Calvary, there they crucified him, and the malefactors, one on the right hand, and the other on the left.(34) Then said Jesus, Father, forgive them; for they know not what they do. And they parted his raiment, and cast lots.(35)And the people stood beholding. And the rulers also with them derided him, saying, He saved others; let him save himself, if he be Christ, the chosen of God.(36)And the soldiers also mocked him, coming to him, and offering him vinegar,(37)And saying, If thou be the king of the Jews, save thyself.(38)And a superscription also was written over him in letters of Greek, and Latin, and Hebrew, THIS IS THE KING OF THE JEWS.(39)And one of the malefactors which were hanged railed on him, saying, If thou be Christ, save thyself and us.(40)But the other answering rebuked him, saying, Dost not thou fear God, seeing thou art in the same condemnation?(41)And we indeed justly; for we receive the due reward of our deeds: but this man hath done nothing amiss.(42)And he said unto Jesus, Lord, remember me when thou comest into thy kingdom.(43)And Jesus said unto him, Verily I say unto thee, To day shalt thou be with me in paradise.(44)And it was about the sixth hour, and there was a darkness over all the earth until the ninth hour.(45)And the sun was darkened, and the veil of the temple was rent in the midst.(46) And when Jesus had cried with a loud voice, he said, Father, into thy hands I commend my spirit: and having said thus, he gave up the ghost.(47) Now when the centurion saw what was done, he glorified God, saying, Certainly this was a righteous man.(48) And all the people that came together to that sight, beholding the things which were done, smote their breasts, and returned.(49)And all his acquaintance, and the women that followed *him from Galilee, stood afar off, beholding these things."*

God knew we needed Jesus to save us from all the world's generational curses, habits, worldly ways, the curse from the garden, and sin. This mighty sacrifice is not an event that should be considered as nothing or counted as little. Jesus, who was completely innocent, naturally and before God, experienced all those hard things and death for the entire world's salvation. Could you stand in a crowd of people and be lied on and beat on for someone else and not utter a word? What about for yourself? Let's be honest, when we are offended, hurt, or even lied on, we respond with the intent to secure our innocence and most of the time the response is not silence and it definitely doesn't come in with a humble spirit with a side of love. We would not let someone spit on us or even hit us knowing our innocence, the natural instinct is to defend ourselves, right. Also, we draw lines in the sand and often mishandle people when we are done wrong, therefore we are not even innocent before the eyes of God because the condition of the heart and mind when we respond. Therefore, he did something for us that we would not do for our own selves. It takes a supernatural strength to bear such a weight. It takes an unexplainable and unconditional love to do such a task.

How amazing is it that he even saves us from ourselves as well, we too experience our eyes being open just as Adam and Eve did, when we allow ourselves to be tempted by the enemy and operate opposite of what God's word says. When Satan comes into our minds and make us question the very righteousness of God, but because we tend to lean to how we feel and our self-desires that does not include God, we fall in the trap of temptation and fall. Which oftentimes we see the effect and point fingers at everyone else but self. We even have the nerve to blame God or ask him why he allowed something to happen not acknowledging it was one's self or even the fault of a generational demonic attachment that brought on the problem. So, for the cause of a dying world (humankind) that was in debt to God, Jesus came to restore the relationship between humankind and God by paying the price for our sins by sacrificing himself as an offering to God so that we who did the sin could be forgiven and not receive the deserved punishment. And he did it before you were even born, he had you in mind. His sacrifice established an everlasting covering that continues for generations that accept him, Jesus Christ as their personal savior until this world ends.

Think of it as this: Imagine going your whole life saving lives as a physician and one day you decide to go out and party and become drunk and you kill someone. Then finding yourself in front of a judge about to receive your deserved punishment for the life you took and the only defense you had was the list of lives you saved at work. Knowing that justice is needed for the one life that was taken by result of your unwise decision. It would not be true justice if the judge did not punish you for the life you took, right? Because a price must be paid for the life taken, justice must be served…. But imagine someone who the judge favors and knows to be innocent and righteous coming in saying charge it to me, ill do the time and take on the punishment for him/her and you walk free from that death penalty. JUSTICE SERVED!

This is the very thing Jesus did for every person. The sins you have personally committed cannot go without eternal punishment. But God allowed Jesus to leave heaven and take on flesh in this wicked world so that those who are willing to come into agreement with him will have a way out into freedom and receive all the promises of God and eternal life. 2 Corinthians 5:21 says, *"For he hath made him to be sin for us, who knew no sin; that we might be made the righteousness of God in him."* Salvation is a gift from God and like any gift from a loved one, it should be valued. But the difference between this gift and a natural gift, the gift is more precious than anything you will find on this world, and it saves your soul. Take a moment and consider your sins and where you have fallen short of the righteousness of God. Evaluate your mind and your heart. How you feel about people and situations, have you forgiven those who hurt or offended you. How are your words, are they fowl and negative? How do you treat others...? Evaluate yourself and write down where you have sinned and think about the innocent blood that was shed for what you have done.

Scripture(s) For Encouragement

"For the wages of sin is death; but the gift of God is eternal life through Jesus Christ our Lord."
Romans 6:23

"For God so loved the world, that he gave his only begotten Son, that whosoever believeth in him should not perish, but have everlasting life." John 3:16

"Neither is there salvation in any other: for there is none other name under heaven given among men, whereby we must be saved." Acts 4:12

"But God commendeth his love towards us, in that, while we

were yet sinners Christ died for us." Romans 5:8

"He that believeth on the Son hath everlasting life." John 3:36

"For if, when we were enemies, we were reconciled to God by the death of his Son, much more, being reconciled, we shall be saved by his life." Romans 5: 10

"And ye know that he was manifested to take away our sins; and in him is no sin." 1 John 3:5

The Apology

God wants to forgive anyone that comes to him sincerely, but the only way to access that forgiveness is by accepting Jesus Christ as your personal savior, Jesus says in John 10:9, "I am the door: by me if any man enter in, he shall be saved, and shall go in and out, and find pasture." There is a great promise once you make it through the door, but the only way to come to Jesus and be accepted into the kingdom is by repentance. YOU MUST FIRST REPENT, Repentance is simply admitting your wrong, apologizing, and changing. True repentance requires remorse, when a person is remorseful there is a deep regret for the wrong, they have done. And when you feel remorseful it is less likely that you would hurt the ones you love again intentionally, you avoid hurting them. Your repentance must be true. Take 10 minutes and consider all your sins you have written down and the ways of God and be honest with how you feel about the wrong you are doing or have done that goes unrepented for. Are you truly sorry for those sins? Are you willing to stop without excuses, right now? Are you willing to surrender completely right now, without excuses?

Knowing the sacrifice Jesus has made to become the mediator between you and God, are you remorseful about your sins? 1 John 1:8-9 says, *"If we say that we have no sin, we deceive ourselves, and the truth is not in us. (9) If we confess our sins, he is faithful and just to forgive us our sins, and to cleanse us from all unrighteousness."* There's hope for you, admitting your sin will require that you become vulnerable and honest with yourself.

Imagine someone calling you and telling you they are coming over and they are going to stay with you while they are in town. Well like most people, you go into cleaning mode, because your house looks a mess in your eyes and you do not want anyone coming to your home and seeing it that way, right. So, you clean and go the extra mile so that everything looks magazine ready. And while they stay, you're on your p's and q's and making sure they have everything they need and that everything looks beautiful. Even their habits that you are not use too, you ignore because it is a part of being hospitable. But let's say something comes up and your guest has to stay a little longer than expected. Well as much as you try in yourself to keep everything beautiful, eventually you start unconsciously exposing your habits, so your guest is no longer experiencing your home as they were before, So the real you start to be revealed. Your real habits start to show, even your character comes through. It's exhausting caring a false sense of reality and living a lie.

Vulnerability allows you see yourself where you are. See vulnerability often comes as a result of exhaustion. So, are you tired? Tired of feeling chained to habits and infirmities that's actually hurting you rather than helping you. Tired of walking in fear that's holding you in bondage. Tired of accepting the life that the world says you must have according to its standards. Tired of feeling depleted when you have tried in all your strengths. Tired of going back and forth in your mind about the past. Tired of fighting this battle with sin on your own. Are you ready to be honest about the dark feelings you are carrying within your heart about someone? Rather it be hate, malice, envy, jealousy, or unforgiveness. Are you ready to admit you do not believe as you say you do? Whatever your sin, whatever you're dealing with, God is not afraid of your confession. He wants you to bring it to him willingly so that he can set you free from those things that's hurting you. Although he sees everything and knows everything, your admittance is a sincere act that says you want to completely depend on God, because it is too much for you to handle on your own. It says, I surrender! John 8:32 says that *"the truth shall make you free"*. Who's truth? Your confession and the truth that you will know, and trust is God's word. You must be honest with what you are dealing with. Sin is a master over you if you allow it, Jesus tells us in John 8:34," *Whosoever committeth sin is the servant of sin."* That lets everyone know that sin comes to control you and the only way to be set free from sin is through Jesus Christ.

Take a moment to evaluate your circumstance and self and be honest if you are willing to be vulnerable. There are many benefits to vulnerability, another being able to grow as a person and finding satisfaction in the relationship between you and God. It is time to relinquish your fears and build the trust by being honest with yourself, because God knows you and all that is in your past and present. Most importantly he knows what your future holds when you surrender everything over to him and trust his words. It is time that you walk away from the past and from every sin that is ultimately hurting you and walk with a deeper love, understanding, and bond with God. This can be established by sincerely repenting, never returning to the old habits and mentality established by sin, solely relying on God's word to be your guide and your life's manual. Paul tells us in Romans 6:1-14, *"What shall we say then? Shall we continue in sin, that grace may abound? (2) God forbid. How shall we, that are dead to sin, live any longer therein? (3) Know ye not, that so many of us as were baptized into*

Jesus Christ were baptized into his death? (4) Therefore we are buried with him by baptism into death: that like as Christ was raised up from the dead by the glory of the Father, even so we also should walk in newness of life. (5) For if we have been planted together in the likeness of his death, we shall be also in the likeness of his resurrection: (6) Knowing this, that our old man is crucified with him, that the body of sin might be destroyed, that henceforth we should not serve sin. (7) For he that is dead is freed from sin.(8) Now if we be dead with Christ, we believe that we shall also live with him:(9) Knowing that Christ being raised from the dead dieth no more; death hath no more dominion over him.(10) For in that he died, he died unto sin once: but in that he liveth, he liveth unto

God. (11)Likewise reckon ye also yourselves to be dead indeed unto sin, but alive unto God through Jesus Christ our Lord. (12)Let not sin therefore reign in your mortal body, that ye should obey it in the lusts thereof. (13) Neither yield ye your members as instruments of unrighteousness unto sin: but yield yourselves unto God, as those that are alive from the dead, and your members as instruments of righteousness unto God.(14)For sin shall not have dominion over you: for ye are not under the law, but under grace." Your sins are completely forgiven, and your surrendering allows Jesus access to your heart and mind for spiritual transformation to take place so that you may walk as a new person. I must also warn you so that you will not fall again, the bible also tells us in Hebrews 6:4-6, *"For* it is *impossible for those who were once enlightened, and have tasted of the heavenly gift, and were made partakers of the Holy Ghost,(5) And have tasted the good word of God, and the powers of the world to come,*

(6)If they shall fall away, to renew them again unto repentance; seeing they crucify to themselves the Son of God afresh, and put him to an open shame." Remember, you should not return to you sins because if you do it is crucifying Jesus again and bringing shame to him.

In addition to the many benefits in having a true relationship with God and his son Jesu you don't have to worry about being reminded about your past sins. In earthly relationships your use to being around people who say they forgive you, but in a moment of anger they throw everything back in your face from the past. It is possible that you too have been one of those unforgiving people, living by the world's motto, "I forgive, but I won't forget". However, God is not *like the bible says in Psalm 103: 8-12, "The LORD is merciful and gracious, slow to anger, and plenteous in mercy.(9) He will not always chide: neither will he keep his anger for ever.(10) He hath not dealt with us after our sins; nor rewarded us according to our iniquities.(11) For as the heaven is high above the earth, so great is his mercy toward them that fear him.(12)As far as the east is from the west, So far has He removed our transgressions from us."*

Your decisions up to this point has kept you from truly having a strong relationship with God and now is the time to establish a stronger and better relationship than before. He has not allowed you to make it through this far without being able to get victory out of those decisions. But you must give him complete access to be in charge over your life. So, no matter how great the sin, GOD IS GREATER. This is the moment that you can posture your heart to be open for the newness of life that comes with repentance and accepting Jesus as your personal savior now that you fully understand what he has done for you personally. Say this prayer of repentance.

Prayer

Father, I come to you with a sincere heart
asking for forgiveness of my sins, I fully
understand what Jesus has done for me and the
sins ive committed. Forgive me for my pride, my
sins, and for thinking I can make it without you.
Forgive me for not allowing you access to my
heart and my mind and for not letting you be
the Lord over my life. I accept Jesus as my
personal savior, and I ask that you be Lord over
my life. Every area that has a spot or any such
blemish please remove it and give me a new
life.
In the name of Jesus Christ,
Amen.

Scripture(s) For Encouragement

"If we confess our sins, he is faithful and just to forgive us our sins, and to cleanse us from all unrighteousness." 1 John 1:9

"For the grace of God that bringeth salvation hath appeared to all men, teaching us that, denying ungodliness and worldly lusts, we should live soberly, righteously, and godly, in this present world." Titus 2:11-12

"Repent ye therefore, and be converted, that your sins may be blotted out, when the times of refreshing shall come from the presence of the Lord." Acts 3:19

"The Lord is not slack concerning his promise, as some men count slackness; but is longsuffering to us- ward, not willing that any should perish, but that all should come to repentance." 2 Peter 3:9

"And the times of this ignorance God winked at; but now commandeth all men every where to repent." Acts 17:30

"If my people, which are called by my name, shall humble themselves, and pray, and seek my face, and turn from their wiced ways; then will I hear from heaven, and will forgive their sin, and will heal their land." 2 Chronicles 7:14

"I tell you, Nay: but, except ye repent, ye shall all likewise perish." Luke 13:3

"Remember therefore from whence thou art fallen, and repent, and do the first works; or else I will come unto thee quickly, and will remove thy candlestick out of his place, except thou repent." Revelation 2:5

Who Is God?

"In the beginning was the Word, and the Word was with God, and the Word was God." John 1:1

God the Creator

God is a Spirit (**John 4:24**), he is not a human being. God is also the creator of everything and everyone, everything exists because he exists. In **Genesis 1:1**, the bible tells us, *"In the beginning **God** created the heaven and the earth."* Further on in **Genesis 2:7**, the bible tells us how God created man, *"And the Lord **God** formed man of the dust of the ground, and breathed into his nostrils the breath of life; and the man became a living soul."* and further in **Genesis 2:21-23** the creation of woman was reveal, " (21)And the Lord God caused a deep sleep to fall upon Adam, and he slept: and he took one of his ribs, and closed up the flesh instead thereof;(22)And the rib, which the Lord God had taken from man, made he a woman, and brought her unto the man. (23) And Adam said, This is now bone of my bones, and flesh of my flesh: she shall be called Woman, because she was taken out of Man."

In Genesis chapter 1 & 2 you will learn that God is the creator of everything by simply speaking it into existence and how he created every being including man and woman, which is why he is called Jehovah Elohim, which means strong creator. Since the beginning of time, the world and people have increased and not only because people but because God is the strong creator. What he speaks could only begin with his word and can only cease at his spoken command.

GOD IS THE CREATOR. He created you in the beginning when he created everything. It wasn't in the time of consumption that he thought of you but in the beginning when he spoke everything in the spirit. Genesis 1: 26-28 says, *"And God said, Let us make man in our image, after our likeness: and let **them** have dominion over the fish of the sea, and over the fowl of the air, and over the cattle, and over all the earth, and over every creeping thing that creepeth upon the earth. (27) So God created man in his image, in the image of God created he **them**. (28) And God blessed **them**, and God said unto* *them, Be fruitful, and multiply, and replenish the earth, and subdue it: and have dominion over the fish of the sea, and over the fowl of the air, and over every living thing that moveth upon the earth."*

Don't be mistaken, this moment in time was before Adam was formed from the dust of the ground (Scripture Reference Genesis Chapter 2). God had each and every person in mind, he not only spoke of your existence, but he assigned purpose at that very moment as well and when he completed all his work he said "behold" which means to see and observe and God said, "it was very good" (Genesis 1:31),he took time to observe all that he spoke into existence and not only called it good, but he said it was very good which means he was extremely pleased with his work and that no evil or corruption was found. So, know that you're not a mistake and nothing about you is a mistake, for at the beginning of creation God declared you good. Further research has revealed that, good in Greek is defined as holy, pure, and righteous. This is the core of who you are being made in the image and likeness of God our Father.

GOD IS YOUR CREATOR and to be made in the the image of him means that you are a holy, pure, and righteous visual representation that's of him in the flesh. It means that he has given you by spirit his personality and morality. How amazing is that! To have a father who spoke nations out his mouth, who purposely made us all look so different but, in the spirit, if we are aligned and connected with him, we are all identical because of his spirit and likeness. In addition, we have the ability to produce what he produces and move what he moves and stop what he stops. What an amazing father! This is the foundation that God established at the beginning, and this is the foundation that has been restored and promised to you once you truly accept Jesus as your personal savior and deny yourself so that you may walk in the spirit.

It's natural to give all the credit to your parents and miss God's hands and his involvement in your existence, but God is where you began. It was God who gave the seed to man, who then planted the seed in the woman who God formed and instilled a womb that's designed to provide safety and time for development in order to birth you, who he spoke into existence in the beginning. God loves you and it's important that you know this, so that you can establish a solid relationship with him as your father.

Scripture(s) For Encouragement

"He hath made the earth by his power, he hath established the world by his wisdom, and hath stretched out the heavens by his discretion." Jeremiah 10:12

"Ah Lord GOD! Behold, thou hast made the heaven and the earth by thy great power and stretched out arm, and there is nothing too hard for thee:"

Jeremiah 32:17

"All things were made by him; and without him was not any thing made that was made." John 1:3

'For by him were all things created, that are in heaven, and that are in earth, visible and invisible, whether they be thrones, or dominions, or principalities, or powers: all things were created by him, and for him:" Colossians 1:16

"Thou art worthy, O Lord, to receive glory and honour and power: for thou hast created all things, and for thy pleasure they are and were created."

Revelation 4:11

God the Father

"For ye have not received the spirit of bondage again to fear, but ye have received the Spirit of adoption, whereby we cry, Abba, Father."

Romans 8:15

Jesus came into the world and through his life and word's showed God as his father. The day that Jesus went to the Jordan to be baptized by John the Baptist (Matthew 3:13-17) God's voice from heaven said, "This is my beloved Son, in whom I am well pleased". This is another level in the relationship that God wants every child to experience with him, to have a personal intimate relationship as son or daughter, in who he can be pleased with. So, what makes you a child of God?

Mark 3:31-35 says, "There came then his brethren and his mother, and, standing without, sent unto him, calling him. (32) And the multitude sat about him, and they said unto him, Behold, thy mother and thy brethren without seek for thee. (33) And he answered them saying, Who is my mother, or my brethren? (34) And he looked round about on them which sat about him, and said, Behold my mother and my brethren! (35) For whosoever shall do the will of God, the same is my brother, and my sister, and mother. "

The key to knowing if you're a child of God is if you are doing the will of God.

What's the will of God? God's will start with the standard for his children and each child must align with God's standard. The standard must be met, and it starts with a simple foundation, if God's children miss the foundational necessities, you will not be able to please God. Consider the foundation of a home. If the foundation of the home is not solid and damages are present, those foundational issues will cause structural issues, such as cracked walls, cracked floor, issues with doors, windows and even plumbing, and over time if not addressed and the issues increase the home will collapse. Let's go into the word to discover the foundation for God's children.

Matthew 22:34-40 says, "But when the Pharisees had heard that he had put the Sadducees to silence, they were gathered together. (35) Then one of them, which was a lawyer, asked him a question, tempting him, and saying, (36) Master, which is the great commandment in the law? (37) Jesus said unto him, thou shalt love the Lord thy God with all thy heart, and with all thy soul, and with all thy mind. (38) This is the first commandment. (39) And the second is like unto it, thou shalt love thy neighbor as thyself. (40) On these two commandments hang all the law and the prophets."

God's will start with love. Loving him with all your heart, soul, and mind. And loving your neighbor as yourself. This may sound so simple, but love is something that many people including those who proclaim to be Christian's struggle with. Because the world has tried to redefine love based on how an individual feels or their experience with someone or lack of experience, but you will discover what it truly means to love God's way. In the word you will discover what it means to love him and what it means and looks like to love your neighbor as yourself. To have a successful relationship with God you must be willing to evaluate your foundation and if any issues are found be willing to acknowledge, correct, and resolve those foundational issues. Remember, if the issues go unaddressed, they will eventually show up in other areas and unaddressed foundational issues results in not living for and pleasing God.

Loving God with Your Heart

Now that you have discovered what the foundational requirements are let's discover what God has to say about the heart and dive into what it means to love God with your heart.

Jeremiah 17:9-10 says, "The heart is deceitful above all things, and desperately wicked: who can know it? (10) I the Lord search the heart, I try the reins, even to give every man according to his ways, and according to the fruit of his doings." Then if you go to the New Testament Jesus tells us in Matthew 15:18-20, "But those things which proceed out of the mouth come forth from the heart; and they defile the man. (19) For out of the heart proceed evil thoughts, murders, adulteries, fornications, thefts, false witness, blasphemies: (20) These are the things which defile a man:"

God doesn't take our word, he looks at the condition of our heart, as you read the scripture, he searches our heart. That's why when many people sin, they would say, "God knows my heart" to excuse the wrong that they have done as if their heart has pure intentions, but they indeed are correct, he knows their heart therefore he is not pleased. Because if most people are honest, when an individual tries within themselves they always result in sin and relaying on their feelings and iniquities, and often times excuse the wrong spoken or done because of one's feelings within, but if you are willing to love God with your heart you must be willing to surrender your heart to him. You must be willing and sincere about going to him and asking for a heart change, it's the only way your heart is going to change. Your relationship with God requires a new heart and this is where you have a spiritual transformation, being born again. Psalm 51: 10-12 says, "Create in me a clean heart, O God; And renew a right spirit within me. (11) Cast me not away from thy presence; And take not thy holy spirit from me. (12) Restore unto me the joy of thy salvation." Here is David a man of God asking for God to give him a new heart. Do you know why he asked? One, desperation, he discovered he alone wasn't capable and two, he knew God could do it because he knew the history and power of God and that God was fully capable to do any and everything. He discovered he needed God to transform him in order to walk this life and succeed this life and he was willing and ready to obey. Even if you take a look at the children of Israel in Ezekiel when God looked out and on behalf of his own name he renewed the people of Israel because they were corrupt and polluted by iniquities and sins but they carried his name and for the sake of his name he told them, "A new heart also will I give you, and a new Spirit will I put with you: and I will take away the stony heart out of your flesh, and I will give you an heart of flesh." He will do the same for you, changing your heart is not something you can do by yourself, it's something that only God can do. Let's look at one of God's greatest heart transformations in the bible, Paul. Paul was named Saul and he was known for persecuting Christians, but one day he had a life changing encounter with Jesus that changed his life. "And Saul, yet breathing out threatenings and slaughter against the disciples of the Lord, went unto the high priest,(2)And desired of him letters to Damascus to the synagogues, that if he found any of this way, whether they were men or women, he might bring them bound unto Jerusalem.(3)And as he journeyed, he came near Damascus: and suddenly there shined round about him a light from heaven:(4)And he fell to the earth, and heard a voice saying unto him, Saul, Saul, why persecutest thou me?(5)And he said, Who art thou, Lord? And the Lord said, I am Jesus whom thou persecutest: *it is* hard for thee to kick against the pricks.(6)And he trembling and astonished said, Lord, what wilt thou have me to do? And the Lord *said* unto him, Arise, and go into the city, and it shall be told thee what thou must do.(7)And the men which journeyed with him stood speechless, hearing a voice, but seeing no man.(8)And Saul arose from the earth; and when his eyes were opened, he saw no man: but they led him by the hand, and brought *him* into Damascus.(9)And he was three days without sight, and neither did eat nor drink.(10)And there was a certain disciple at Damascus, named Ananias; and to him said the Lord in a vision, Ananias. And he said, Behold, I *am here*, Lord.(11)And the Lord *said* unto him, Arise, and go into the street which is called Straight, and enquire in the house of Judas for *one* called Saul, of Tarsus: for, behold, he prayeth,(12)And hath seen in a vision a man named Ananias coming in, and putting *his* hand on him, that he might receive his sight.(13)Then Ananias answered, Lord, I have heard by many of this man, how much evil he hath done to thy saints at Jerusalem:(14)And here he hath authority from the chief priests to bind all that call on thy name.(15)But the Lord said unto him, Go thy way: for he is a chosen vessel unto me, to bear my name before the Gentiles, and kings, and the children of Israel:(16)For I will shew him how great things he must suffer for my name's sake.(17)And Ananias went his way, and entered into the house; and putting his hands on him said, Brother Saul, the Lord, *even* Jesus, that appeared unto thee in the way as thou camest, hath sent me, that thou mightest receive thy sight, and be filled with the Holy Ghost.(18)And immediately there fell from his eyes as it had been scales: and he received sight forthwith, and arose, and was baptized."

Can you imagine the heart of a man that approved the killing of the Saints? A man with the purpose to be completely against the church, to bound them, and stop them. That's a dark heart with hatred for the body, but it took for him to encounter Jesus for his life to be immediately changed. Notice how when the light shined it blinded him and bought him to his knees, he was humbled. He addressed Jesus as Lord before he knew it was Jesus, see how humility will allow you to recognize authority even if you aren't very clear as to who's speaking or what's going on. This encounter made him surrender willingly. Though he was humbled he was also trembling and astonished, but he also felt something he never felt before, the love of Christ because it is impossible to be in his presence and not feel his love. Although he was being reprimanded, he knew it was for his good. He was willing to hand over his agenda and life in a matter of 3 sentences, how amazing is that. Only true love can make you surrender and change in an instance. In addition, he understood Jesus when he said, "It is hard for thee to kick against the pricks". A prick is a stick with a piece of iron on its tip, it was used to steer the animal in the right direction and if the animal resisted by kicking out at the prick the prick would automatically be driven further into its flesh causing it to suffer more. So, Paul understood that if he continued down the road of persecuting Jesus, the Christians, he was going to suffer more. Remember his sight was taken away from him, so could you imagine your life taking a sudden change downhill and knowing its only going to get worse. Therefore, he responded with, "what will thou have me to do?"

This is how anyone should feel when they truly encounter the love of Jesus, the saving love he has for us. Paul could have chosen to continue doing what he was trained to do but he chose to surrender. Your flesh is made to fight against anything its iniquity taught it, but nothing can fight and overcome Jesus and his love. Your encounter may not look identical to Paul's, but in your life, you too have made some decisions that says in action that you are against Christ. Your disobedience and rejection of righteousness is as persecuting Jesus. But you too have grace for salvation. With your complete surrender, God has access to restore your heart, to give you a new heart that will change your life forever. It's your job to refuse the enemy and your flesh and operate in what God said, your heart should mirror the heart of God. The way that you know you love God with your heart is when you obey his word no matter what. When opposition comes in many forms you are slow in anger and quicker to hear and pray. You become quick to rely on God's word and directions rather that your thoughts and emotions. There's grace for you to align with the word of God and his will. For the message to you is the same, if you continue to kick against the pricks, you too will suffer. Give God access, deny your feelings, your iniquities, and allow him to change your heart. It's easy to go back to what you rely on, but its also easy to choose Jesus and follow God's way. Jesus' love is a love that confounds the world but to those that truly understand the love he has for them, they all his love to consume them and change them.

Prayer

Father, forgive me for not loving you with all of my heart. I have put my feelings and my opinion before your word, and I am sorry. I have allowed my feelings and the influence of the world to be Lord over my life instead of you. I have not obeyed your every word, I repent for my disobedience, and I come to you now asking in Jesus' name, for a new heart. Change my heart and give me a new heart as you said in your word, Lord I am your child and I pray for your name's sake that you will have the same mercy on me and wash me of all iniquities and remove my stony heart and give me a heart of flesh.

In Jesus name I ask,

Amen

Loving God with Your Mind

This mental transformation is going to cause for you to be different and separated from the world and the ways of the world. You are going to have to remove your conditioned mind, the way you've been taught through life by the world and its system and allow God to teach you a new thing with unlimited possibilities.

God wants you to see him as father because he is the life giver but, he is so much more, and he desires that you get to experience him and life with him. The father will love you as well as teach you, give you a good life, protect you, provide for you, discipline you, when necessary, he also wants to spend time with you, and cover you, but it's going to require for you to see life as he sees it without your additives. The only way you're going to access the good and peaceful life is by relinquishing your mind completely.

Romans 12:2 says, "And be not conformed to this world: but be ye transformed by the renewing of your mind, that ye may prove what is that good, and acceptable, and perfect, will of God." Your mind controls how you operate, ultimately your flesh. Read about Zacchaeus, a rich man that did not rely on his resources but in desperation was willing to see Jesus and give of his earthly possessions in abundance to be saved. Let's see how he did not rely on his normal thinking to obtain salvation. "And *Jesus* entered and passed through Jericho.(2)And, behold, *there was* a man named Zacchaeus, which was the chief among the publicans, and he was rich.(3)And he sought to see Jesus who he was; and could not for the press, because he was little of stature.(4)And he ran before, and climbed up into a sycomore tree to see him: for he was to pass that *way*.(5)And when Jesus came to the place, he looked up, and saw him, and said unto him, Zacchaeus, make haste, and come down; for to day I must abide at thy house.(6)And he made haste, and came down, and received him joyfully.(7)And when they saw *it*, they all murmured, saying, That he was gone to be guest with a man that is a sinner.(8)And Zacchaeus stood, and said unto the Lord; Behold, Lord, the half of my goods I give to the poor; and if I have taken any thing from any man by false accusation, I restore him fourfold. (9)And Jesus said unto him, This day is salvation come to this house, forsomuch as he also is a son of Abraham.(10)For the Son of man is come to seek and to save that which was lost." (Luke 19:1-10)

Zacchaeus may have been a short man in height, but he held a prominent position as a toll and tax collector, he was rich. Zacchaeus in spite of his position and money, did not use neither to get through the crowds of people. He actually prepared to see Jesus by going ahead of the crowd and climbing up a tree. See he went against his natural instinct and in desperation he climbs the sycomore tree to see Jesus. And in that, Jesus looked up and saw him and from there he was able to abide with Jesus in his home. The world teaches, use your position and money to get an advantage over people to get what you want, but the only way you are going to get to experience Jesus is if you apply the same method that Zacchaeus did. Thinking outside what you have been taught to do. God's way does not look like the world's way, when you are desperate and willing to do what God says, something others aren't doing, you in return will always reap a good thing. Look at how the people around were talking because they were shocked to see Jesus go with a sinner, they had expectations, but as you read they talked and Jesus didn't stop and say no you're a sinner the people are talking, I can't go, Jesus was about doing the will of the Father. Jesus knew his purpose and he didn't change his mind in spite of people. In addition, Zacchaeus mind was not the only thing that was different, his heart was, and it showed through his willingness to give half of his goods to the poor and in his willingness to right his wrongs. Because of his desperation and willingness, he was able to encounter Jesus and salvation for not just him but his entire house. No one else was climbing trees, are you willing to climb a tree to encounter Jesus? Are you prepared to go ahead of the crowd so that your family will be saved? Are you willing to right your wrongs and give yourself? It's going to require your mind to be different and committed to seeing God. Seeing what he says and not altering the plan despite of adversity.

The only way you can get control over your flesh and reject your worldly mentality is by being led by the spirit of God and walking in the spirit. Walking in the spirit is when you observe and respond from the spiritual understanding of heaven rather than rely on your natural understanding and instinct. God has a Spirit that allows his children to have InSite above natural understanding. When you surrender your mind and take on the Spirit of God there's proof in your actions and within yourself. The word tells us in Galatians 5:22-23, "But the fruit of the Spirit is love, joy, peace, longsuffering, gentleness, goodness, faith, meekness, temperance." So, when your mind is transformed these are the results of a transformed mind that is being led by the Spirit of God. In order to love God with your mind you must surrender your mind.

This is how you become the new creation that the word speaks of in 2 Corinthians 5:17, "Therefore if any man be in Christ, he is a new creature: old things are passed away; behold, all things are become new. "The new things are all things pertaining to God, new heart, new mind, and new spirit, all that's righteous and holy. Your knowledge once under the authority of the Father should be based after holiness and righteousness, because he gives you understanding and wisdom that confounds the world and the world operates as an enemy to God. Loving God with your mind looks like you are taking on his character and his system, the way that he meant for you to be from the beginning.

Prayer

Father, I pray that you transform me completely. I want to love you in every way necessary so that I can be all that you designed me to be. I surrender my mind to you, and I pray for holy boldness to stand no matter what the world says or no matter who comes against me. Give me the strength to stand boldly for you. Forgive me for not loving you as I should have been. Father, you can have me, I surrender my heart, mind, and soul to you. Have your way, I am yours, use me for your glory.

In Jesus name I pray.

Amen

What's Love? -Loving Your Neighbor

Jesus gave us instructions for abiding in the will of the father and it did not only include you and only God but his will include you and everyone around you. Your relationship with God doesn't' include just you and him but he wanted to make sure no one was left out. God has no respect of person and since we all come from him, he has a standard that we must love and respect everyone. For the simple yet powerful basis that he created them and if you love him and respect him, you must love and respect what comes from him. 1 John 4:20 says, "If a man say, I love God, and hateth his brother, he is a liar: for he that loveth not his brother who he hath seen, how can he love God whom he hath not seen?" You have the responsibility to love everyone and not according to how you feel but according to the word and the word tells us in 1 Corinthians 13:4-8 what love is exactly. "Charity suffereth long, *and* is kind; charity envieth not; charity vaunteth not itself, is not puffed up,(5) Doth not behave itself unseemly, seeketh not her own, is not easily provoked, thinketh no evil;(6) Rejoiceth not in iniquity, but rejoiceth in the truth;(7)Beareth all things, believeth all things, hopeth all things, endureth all things. Charity never faileth."(Read scripture in NIV for clarity) Take a moment and really consider this definition God gives us and consider anyone you're at odds with or how you treat people rather you know them or not. This is love and anything opposite of it is not love. See many times our flesh says, "I love them" but there's many excuses that follow or actions that draws a line in the sand. Not loving your neighbor God's way is unacceptable. When you do not love everyone like God says you are not doing his will. And if you are not doing his will, you have not taken on the relationship through Jesus as a child of God. If you love God, you MUST love your neighbor also.

As a servant of God, who works in the ministry, it is better to have a perfect foundation than you operate in all your wonderful gifts. The bible says in 1 Corinthians 13:2-5, " And though I have the gift of prophecy, and understand all mysteries, and all knowledge; and though I have all faith, so that I could remove mountains, and have not charity, I am nothing. (3) And though I bestow all my goods to feed the poor, and though I give my body to be burned, and have not charity, it profiteth me nothing." So, as the bible says, love covers a multitude of sin, but it also allows us to operate in the ministry without having to hear Jesus say depart from me. Your heart must be conditioned to love as God has said you should love. That would be a hard and hurtful fall, to do all that work and be turned away because you couldn't fulfill the first 2 commandments. Jesus says in Matthew 7:21-23, "Not every one that saith unto me, Lord, Lord, shall enter into the kingdom of heaven; but he that doeth the will of my Father which is in heaven. (22) Many will say to me in that day, Lord, Lord, have we not prophesied in thy name? and in thy name have cast out devils? And in thy name done many wonderful works?

(23) And then will I profess unto them, I never knew you: depart from me, ye that work iniquity." Remember, loving your neighbor is the will of God. Every believer who surrenders their life to Christ has the charge to love God and everyone. Read how Jesus went ahead of his disciples and established a bridge to a group of people were there was division. John 4:1-36, "When therefore the Lord knew how the Pharisees had heard that Jesus made and baptized more disciples than John,(2)(Though Jesus himself baptized not, but his disciples,)(3)He left Judaea, and departed again into Galilee.(4)And he must needs go through Samaria.(5)Then cometh he to a city of Samaria, which is called Sychar, near to the parcel of ground that Jacob gave to his son

Joseph.(6)Now Jacob's well was there. Jesus therefore, being wearied with *his* journey, sat thus on the well: *and* it was about the sixth hour.(7)There cometh a woman of Samaria to draw water: Jesus saith unto her, Give me to drink.(8)(For his disciples were gone away unto the city to buy meat.)(9)Then saith the woman of Samaria unto him, How is it that thou, being a Jew, askest drink of me, which am a woman of Samaria? for the Jews have no dealings with the Samaritans.(10)Jesus answered and said unto her, If thou knewest the gift of God, and who it is that saith to thee, Give me to drink; thou wouldest have asked of him, and he would have given thee living water.(11)The woman saith unto him, Sir, thou hast nothing to draw with, and the well is deep: from whence then hast thou that living water?(12)Art thou greater than our father Jacob, which gave us the well, and drank thereof himself, and his children, and his cattle?(13)Jesus answered and said unto her, Whosoever drinketh of this water shall thirst again:(14)But whosoever drinketh of the water that I shall give him shall never thirst; but the water that I shall give him shall be in him a well of water springing up into everlasting life.(15)The woman saith unto him, Sir, give me this water, that I thirst not, neither come hither to draw.(16)Jesus saith unto her, Go, call thy husband, and come hither.(17)The woman answered and said, I have no husband. Jesus said unto her, Thou hast well said, I have no husband:(18)For thou hast had five husbands; and he whom thou now hast is not thy husband:

in that saidst thou truly.(19)The woman saith unto him, Sir, I perceive that thou art a prophet.(20)Our fathers worshipped in this mountain; and ye say, that in Jerusalem is the place where men ought to worship. (21)Jesus saith unto her, Woman, believe me, the hour cometh, when ye shall neither in this mountain, nor yet at Jerusalem, worship the Father.(22)Ye worship ye know not what: we know what we worship: for salvation is of the Jews.(23)But the hour cometh, and now is, when the true worshippers shall worship the Father in spirit and in truth: for the Father seeketh such to worship him.(24)God *is* a Spirit: and they that worship him must worship *him* in spirit and in truth.(25)The woman saith unto him, I know that Messias cometh, which is called Christ: when he is come, he will tell us all things.

(26)Jesus saith unto her, I that speak unto thee am *he*.(27)And upon this came his disciples, and marvelled that he talked with the woman: yet no man said, What seekest thou? or, Why talkest thou with her?(28)The woman then left her waterpot, and went her way into the city, and saith to the men,(29)Come, see a man, which told me all things that ever I did: is not this the Christ?(30)Then they went out of the city, and came unto him.(31)In the mean while his disciples prayed him, saying, Master, eat.(32)But he said unto them, I have meat to eat that ye know not of.(33)Therefore said the disciples one to another, Hath any man brought him *ought* to eat?(34)Jesus saith unto them, My meat is to do the will of him that sent me, and to finish his work. (35)Say not ye, There are yet four months, and then cometh the harvest? Behold, I say unto you, Lift up your eyes, and look on the fields, for they are white already to harvest. (36)And he that reapeth receiveth wages, and gathereth fruit unto life eternal: that both he that soweth and the that reapeth may rejoice together."

Here you have this Samaritan woman who was speaking with Jesus, a Jew. This is significant because you should know that the Samaritans and the Jews did not associate with one another, they hated each other. Because they held difference of opinions so much so, the Jews called them "half-breeds", it's a long history that goes back to Jacob's children. The hate was so strong that the Jews would not travel through Samaria they would take a longer route to avoid contact. However, the well was made a common ground after this encounter with Jesus. Because Jesus is a loving savior, he loved this woman, and he proved his love to her by offering her the opportunity to be fulfilled through him. He offered her everlasting life, before he told her of her sins, he showed her he was willing to extend an olive branch through that offer. Jesus did not only tell her about her wrong doings, but he also told her about things that only he could, so she was fully convinced. As they were speaking the disciples wondered why Jesus spoke with this Samaritan woman. They expected to return to feed him and move on with their journey, but Jesus was building a bridge between to groups for the purposes that all humankind be saved through love. He prepared the disciples as the woman went back to the city to spread the word. He informed that it was time to extend salvation to all man, he has set the foundation through his encounter with the woman who went to invite the people to come see Jesus. It was time for them to come together so that they could all reap eternal life.

So as a believer, you cannot extend love to whom you please. It goes beyond your close friends and close family. When you become a child of God, you have the responsibility to love and for the purposes of the kingdom, you must show love God's way. Don't worry about being taken advantage of, just simply love with the love of God. It's time to be committed to doing the will of God. No longer should you be operating in hate, the bible says in 1 John 3:15, "Whosoever hateth his brother is a murderer: and ye know that no murderer hath eternal life abiding in him. So no more going the distance to be separated out of hate. You must allow Jesus to go ahead of you just like he did with the Samaritan woman, because only he can soften the heart of any man or woman. Allow Jesus to build the bridge and you walk in the assignment you have, which is the responsibility to harvest, and that's to love.

Prayer

Father, I have not loved my neighbors as you have told me too, forgive me. I have had respect of persons and have operated out of it. I repent for this sin, and I ask that you fill me with the love of Christ. Fill me with the love that's patient, kind, not envious, boastful, or prideful. Let me not dishonor others or be selfish. Remove anger and bitterness from me, so that I keep no record of wrongs. Remind me to never take pleasure in evil but find happiness in truth. Bless me to protect, trust, and always have hope in my neighbors.

In Jesus name,

Amen

Scripture(s) For Encouragement

"A new commandment I give unto you, That ye love one another; as I have loved you, that ye also love one another."
John 13:34

"Owe no man any thing, but to love one another: for he that loveth another hath fulfilled the law." Romans 13:8

"And above all things have fervent charity among yourselves: for charity shall cover the multitude of sins." 1 Peter 4:8

"Hatred stirreth up strifes: but love covereth all sins." Proverbs 10:12

"Beloved, let us love one another: for love is of God; and every one that loveth is born of God, and knoweth God. He that loveth not knoweth not God; for God is love." 1 John 4:7-8

"For all the law is fulfilled in one word, even in this; Thou shalt love thy neighbor as thyself." Galatians 5:14

"But love ye your enemies, and do good, and lend, hoping for nothing again; and your reward shall be great, and ye shall be the children of the Highest: for

he is kind unto the unthankful and to the evil." Luke 6:35

"And we know that all things work together for good to them that love God, to them who are the called according to his purpose." Romans 8:28

"Let love be without dissumlation. Abhor that which is evil; cleave to that which is good." Romans 12:9

TRUST

---

*"Trust in the LORD with all thine
heart; and lean not unto thine
own understanding."*

Provetbs 3:5

Learn to trust God.

Trust is essential in every successful
relationship; without it the relationship will
never grow. Let's take some time to learn about
Abraham's journey in trusting God.

Abraham was called by God to leave out of his

country, leave his family, and all things familiar.

God told Abraham that he was going to make

him a great nation, fruitful, and make his name

great. Later God also promised Abraham an heir

with his wife Sarah. They were the age of one hundred and Sarah ninety at that point. For Abraham to receive the promises of God it required his obedience every step of the way. (For additional, study Genesis Chapters 12-17)

Abraham took a step of faith and obeyed and because of that faith he was able to build a relationship with God as well as learn the character of God. Isn't it amazing how we read about a testimony such as Abraham and it starts when he was 75 years old, and the bible doesn't' give us history concerning any of his past that would have led up to his initial point of encounter? However, whatever his past was, what we do know is that it was not good enough for God to keep him there and the future that God had in store for him was greater than what was present for him. How amazing is it that God's voice was enough for Abraham, it gave him hope. Imagine never knowing someone and they come to you with instructions and promises and their voice was enough for you to move towards the promises. Have you heard the voice of God, and did it give you hope for your future? Abraham left all that he knew in order to obtain a better life and the only way he could have gained all that he gained was through trusting God. Take a moment to read about one occurrence that happened to Abraham and learn about how he trusted God.

Genesis 22:1-19, "And it came to pass after these things, that God did tempt Abraham, and said unto him, Abraham: and he said, Behold, here I am.(2) And he said, Take now thy son, thine only son Isaac, whom thou lovest, and get thee into the land of Moriah; and offer him there for a burnt offering upon one of the mountains which I will tell thee of.(3) And Abraham rose up early in the morning, and saddled his ass, and took two of his young men with him, and Isaac his son, and clave the wood for the burnt offering, and rose up, and went unto the place of which God had told him.(4) Then on the third day Abraham lifted up his eyes, and saw the place afar off.(5) And Abraham said unto his young men, Abide ye here with the ass; and I and the lad will go yonder and worship, and come again to you.(6) And Abraham took the wood of the burnt offering, and laid it upon Isaac his son;

and he took the fire in his hand, and a knife; and they went both of them together.(7)And Isaac spake unto Abraham his father, and said, My father: and he said, Here am I, my son. And he said, Behold the fire and the wood: but where is the lamb for a burnt offering?(8)And Abraham said, My son, God will provide himself a lamb for a burnt offering: so they went both of them together.(9)And they came to the place which God had told him of; and Abraham built an altar there, and laid the wood in order, and bound Isaac his son, and laid him on the altar upon the wood.(10)And Abraham stretched forth his hand, and took the knife to slay his son.(11) And the angel of the LORD called unto him out of heaven, and said, Abraham, Abraham: and he said, Here am I.(12)And he said, Lay not thine hand upon the lad, neither do thou any thing unto him: for now I know that thou fearest God, seeing thou hast not withheld thy son, thine only son from me.(13)And Abraham lifted up his eyes, and looked, and behold behind him a ram caught in a thicket by his horns: and Abraham went and took the ram, and offered him up for a burnt offering in the stead of his son.(14)And Abraham called the name of that place Jehovah jireh: as it is said to this day, In the mount of the LORD it shall be seen.(15) And the angel of the LORD called unto Abraham out of heaven the second time,(16)And said, By myself have I sworn, saith the LORD, for because thou hast done this thing, and hast not withheld thy son, thine only son(17)That in blessing I will bless thee, and in multiplying I will multiply thy seed as the stars of the heaven, and as the sand which is upon the sea shore; and thy seed shall possess the gate of his enemies;(18)And in thy seed shall all the nations of the earth be blessed; because thou hast obeyed my voice.(19) So Abraham returned unto his young men, and they rose up and went together to Beersheba; and Abraham dwelt at Beersheba."

Here they are and God fulfilled his promise, Sarah in her old age gave birth to the promised child. Remember this is the only son they have together, and Abraham is instructed by God to offer Issac for a burnt offering, to basically take the life of Issac and offer his blood as a sacrifice. As read, Abraham gets up the next morning prepared and went on to the place he was instructed. It was a three-day journey and on the third day Abraham said out of his mouth that he and Issac were going to worship and come back. SOUNDS LIKE HE HAD FAITH IN GOD.

But he never questioned God, he still walked as instructed-even when Issac asked where's the lamb for the burnt offering, Abraham's response was "God will provide himself a lamb".

It got as far as Abraham building the alter, bounding Issac, and placing him on the alter and as he stretched forth his hand to slay his promised son, God stopped him.

Abraham trusted God ALL THE WAY. He knew that his obedience was necessary without questioning. He experienced God so much up to that point that he knew the character of God. To bring him out of his land and separate him and be blessed, he experienced talking with God, he experienced God bringing Lot and his family out of Sodom and Gomorrah. So, he knew the history of God had not failed him and that he could trust God. He had faith that even if he had to slay his son, he knew God had provided the son and the son was not ultimately his and he would have been giving back what he only was blessed to experience.

Like any relationship, the only way that someone is willing to trust the words of another person, most of the time the trust must be built up as well as within human relationships we tend to want people to prove themselves or their words proven to be true before trust is given. Note these words in your heart, God CAN be trusted. He is a good father with good intentions. In the word, Jeremiah 29:11 God says, "For I know the plans I have for you, saith the LORD, thoughts of peace, and not of evil, to give you an expected end." God has a plan for you but remember its his plan. And his plan is better than any plan you can have for yourself because God knows every detail past, present, and future. And since he can foresee those details, the plan he has will ultimately protect you, guide you in the right path, and succeed you.

We are the ones that must prove ourselves to him. He has taken so many steps so that you can trust him, so that you can trust his words and not doubt him. Even when you consider the beginning of the world when Adam and Eve disobeyed him, he places Jesus apart of the plan to come in and save every person through his life and sacrifice all to save those that are willing to be saved.

Can you imagine giving up what you know to be a good thing without knowing what the results are going to be, leaving all that you know? God is always talking, God instructs his children through his word, others, life occurrences, and encounters with him and every time excuses are made based off feelings and "common sense", but God didn't ask that you consider those things. Your emotions and common sense, which can be counted as your mentality and the way that you have been trained to think, will get you in trouble every time if you consider those things more dependable than God. What you are doing is relying on your conscience to determine your obedience. God should be the voice that you rely on, no matter what it feels or appears to be. Think back on the last time God gave you instructions, did you obey? Whether the instructions came through a life occurrence, someone that spoke to you, the message you last heard in a service, or read in his word. If you are having a hard time identifying that moment, it's okay. But be aware because the enemy has so many tricks that's purpose is to distract you from those very instructions, and they come in so many forms. Even with believers who are not operating in the Spirit but in distress and offense, its easy to sit amongst the word and point fingers at who you feel the word is for in the crowd, all while missing the word that is for you. In addition, you can miss instructions even when you reject correction in your heart because your flesh is at war with the spirit.

So, the question now is, will you trust God? Will you let go of your plans and release everything you know and allow him to become your teacher and guide? Will you obey him even when you do not feel like it or agree? Knowing what you know about the expected end, will you trust him?

He's in control, Stay focused

Matthew 14: 24-33

"But the ship was now in the midst of the sea, tossed with waves: for the wind was contrary. (25) And in the fourth watch of the night Jesus went unto them, walking on the sea. (26) And when the disciples saw him walking on the sea, the were troubled, saying ,It is spirit; and the cried out for fear. (27) But straightway Jesus spake unto them, saying, Be of good cheer; it is I; be not afraid. (28) And Peter answered him and said, Lord, if it be thou, bed me come unto thee on the water. (29) And he said, Come. And when Peter was come down out of the ship, he walked on the water, to go to Jesus. (30) But when he saw he wind boisterous, he was afraid; and beginning to sink, he cried, saying, Lord, save me. (31) And immediately Jesus stretched forth his hand, and caught him, and said unto him, O thou of little faith, wherefore didst thou doubt? (32) And when they were come into the ship, the wind ceased. (33) Then they that were in the ship came and worshipped him, saying, of a truth thou art the Son of God.

What an amazing and scary situation to be in right? Would you have asked to go to Jesus? Does life feel like a storm for you? And are you having a tough time staying focus on Jesus and all his instructions? One observation I want you to make here is that Jesus never moves, but he did reach out and he caught Peter when he began to sink. Could his stillness be that he was so confident in the authority and power that

God gave him? How great a savior he is, to exemplify such a confidence an power at a horrifying time. You too should take on that same confidence, not in yourself but in God, the Father. So, that when you observe things falling apart around you, you won't be affected by what appears to be threatening.

Jesus doesn't change in this situation- he proves himself to literally come in and fulfill his purpose for being the calm in the storm, showing those that chose to believe in him that he has the authority over the storm no matter what it looks like, what's happening, or how it feels-therefore he is in control. Note, JESUS WAS NOT AFRAID OF THE WINDS AND HOW FAR HE WOULD HAVE HAD TO GO TO GET TO THOSE HE LOVE. Remember, the ship was in the middle of the sea tossed with waves and in tough winds. And just like the situation that we all are a part of concerning this world and the enemy that's out to steal, kill, and destroy. When Satan deceived Eve and sin entered in but in the midst of chaos a world full of sin, Jesus was born and came to our rescue to cancel the curse and lay down his life so that those that believe will have their sins forgiven and access to God through him.

The goal of this passage is that you as the believer who comes to him to trust him. To know that he's in control and when you trust him with your life you will experience life through a miraculous supernatural lens even when regular life appears to be contrary to what God promised.

Let's look at peter in this passage, after Jesus told the disciples to be of good cheer and to not be afraid because it was him. Peter made the request to Jesus to do something he knew only Jesus could do, which was to allow him to come to him **on the water**. Peter believed that Jesus could do it, the history he had with Jesus allowed him to know that Jesus went against everything he, peter, thought he knew. So, the fact that he knew that water could not hold him and that he would sink did not matter, he no longer trusted what he knew, he believed Jesus to be Lord over the water. He removed the conditioned mind and trusted in one source, Jesus. So, because he trusted Jesus, he was able to experience a miracle in the midst of the storm, he walked on the water.

Now you also read that when he saw the boisterous wind, he began to be afraid, and he started to sink while he was on his way walking to Jesus. Many would say he took his eyes off Jesus, but I would like to also add that just for a moment when he saw the winds he took his mind off Jesus, he lost his focus. The point of him even asking to get off the ship was so that he could go to Jesus and for a moment he took notice of the unruly winds around him and in that moment his focus was detoured which allowed fear of the flesh and doubt to creep in. This also applies to every believer, when a believer takes the step to come to Jesus and Satan begins to stir up things in the person's life through people, things, and circumstances and the person loses focus. One begins to put all their focus on what they think they have control over and begin to respond wrongly and out of an emotion or iniquity, but because it's a spiritual battle one loses because the individual tries to fix things naturally. When what should be done is a continuous walk to Christ. What you focus on will show where your trust lies, in you or in Jesus.

One key word in this passage is contrary. The wind was contrary…The world is going to be contrary, the standard of the world and the mentality of those who operate according to the worlds teaching. Even amongst contrary situations you will have to keep your focus on Jesus, by learning and remembering the life he exemplified, by trusting the word of God to be enough for you to believe and live by. No matter what wind comes, your response should be to trust in the word of God and respond only how he tells you too and how he wants you to respond can be found in his written word, which is why it's important to hide the word in your heart. (Scripture ref. Psalm 119: 10-11 "10) With my whole heart have I sought thee: O let me not wander from thy commandments. (11) Thy word have I hid in mine heart, That I might not sin against thee.") That's how you overcome the winds and not sink, anytime we trust in ourselves and the natural ungodly instinct we are going against God, because the flesh can only respond out of sin. But, when you deny how you feel, think, or talk about a situation or person and only think, feel, and speak as God tells you than is when you have chosen to continue to walk to Jesus.

Many often question, if God is in control why does he even allows things to happen. But what we face today is based off the choice made back in the garden to disobey God. Remember God gives free choice, he doesn't want any of his children to love and obey him unwillingly or by force. God wants your love and obedience to be willingly. But as a result of the choice that was made, he sent Jesus to intervene in the storm. The storms are an example of God allowing us to see that even though the storms are going to happen and things are going to come against you, but the key is remembering who is with you and the power that he holds over whatever is coming against you.

You must trust within your mind and heart that there is victory because God is with you, He is undefeated. Once you truly trust that God has already went before you, you will have no reason to fear or doubt because you trust who he is and no other source including yourself.

Prayer

Father, help me to trust you, I have trusted myself and all that I know, although limited. From this moment forward I am choosing to trust you no matter what it looks like, I believe you know all things and have a better plan for me than I have for myself. Forgive me for any doubt that I have had in your word, and I ask that you remove fear from me, so that I may continue my walk with you undistracted. Teach me your ways and be the Lord over my life.

I ask all these things in the name of

Jesus Christ, my savior.

Amen

Scripture(s) For Encouragement

"Commit thy way unto the Lord; trust also in him; and he shall bring it to pass." Psalm 37:5

"Blessed is the man that trusteth in the Lord, and whose hope the Lord is. For he shall be as a tree planted by the waters, and that spreadeth out her roots by the river, and shall not see when heat cometh, but her leaf shall be green; and shall not be careful in the year of drought, neither shall cease from yielding fruit." Jeremiah 17:7-8

"Let not your heart be troubled: ye believe in God, believe also in me." John 14:1

Quality Time

Spending Time with God

To see the value in spending time with God, you must see his value. You must value him and have a heart that desires to please him and the only way your heart is going to be postured in the way to please God is to know who he is, what he does, and why he did it. At this point you should have established a knowing for who God is and a heart that sees his value and knows his value. All relationships require quality time, if there isn't quality time, the relationship will struggle in other areas, and it will not be strong. It's important that you set dedicated time to spend with God.

Quality time with God is giving him your undivided attention. Many people struggle with spending time with God, often with the mind set of inserting God in their schedule and not making him the priority. For example: someone could say, I want to read and study more of the word of God, but I don't have time because I have to work, I have a life, I have children, I have to go to the gym, and I have to cook and clean and other various responsibilities. It's about being dedicated, so what does that look like? Removing all distractions that takes your focus off you learning of him, getting to know who he is, what his character is, and hearing from him. It's like going on a date, you prepare to spend time with the person, and you know when you're on that date you're going to spend time with that person so you most likely will not be answering the telephone, looking on social media, or watching tv. Because your point is to show interest in the person and grow closer to them…. APPLY THAT SAME METHOD WITH GOD

Separate yourself and put away all the distractions set the mood, play worship music that will invite his presence in that will change your heart posture and usher in the spirit of God. Then begin to talk with God and read about him and allow the spirit of God to speak with you and guide you in the word. Don't be afraid to tell God about your day and what you're feeling on the inside. He is not afraid of your feelings nor disappointments; he wants you to bring everything to him so that he can walk you through each problem and emotion. SHARE YOURSELF. Be intentional about there being no interruptions. Give God your undivided attention.

There are different ways to spend time with God. For example, going for a walk and allowing the word to be played in your ears or music and talk with him or creating you a space where there's peace and quiet. There's no restriction on where or how you spend time with God, just make sure you don't pencil him in but that you make him a priority.

When Jesus was on earth, he was intentional about spending time with God, his father. Matthew 14:23 reads, "And when he had sent the multitudes away, he went up into a mountain apart to pray: and when the evening was come, he was there alone." So, Jesus separated himself when he spent time with God, and he didn't just spend a couple of minutes he spent a significant amount of time praying. This is your example of what your quality time should look like with God. Consider even, Martha and Mary, in Luke 10:38-42 it says, " Now it came to pass, as they went, that he entered into a certain village: and a certain woman named Martha received him into her house.(39)And she had a sister called Mary, which also sat at Jesus' feet, and heard his word.(40)But Martha was cumbered about much serving, and came to him, and said, Lord, dost thou not care that my sister hath left me to serve alone? bid her therefore that she help me.(41)And Jesus answered and said unto her, Martha, Martha, thou art careful and troubled about many things: (42)But one thing is needful: and Mary hath chosen that good part, which shall not be taken away from her."

Here you have two women, and one is serving, and one is sitting at the feet of Jesus, Martha was so upset because serving others had gotten the best of her and she had become overwhelmed and wanted Mary to help. But Mary had placed herself in the most important place she could, at the feet of Jesus, soaking in his presence and his every word. The choice Mary had made was not only good, but it was important and in the words of Jesus, "needful". Your time with God is more important than this race in life, which is why it's important that you be intentional about making it the first thing you do daily. This time is "needful" because its where you'll get all your information and direction, its where you can be built up and empowered. Remember to include these three factors to your quality time with God.

- Be Intentional
- Be Alone
- Don't Rush, enjoy God

Take some time and reflect on your quality time with God. Write down what good effective quality time looks like to you. Think about an important relationship in your life and write down how often your you spend time with them and compare it to your quality time with God, your time with God should exceed the time you spend with those you love. Ask yourself this question, AM I SPENDING QUALITY TIME WITH GOD?

What is Prayer

Prayer is simply communicating with God. Your quality time includes prayer. Prayer is spiritual because God is a Spirit and in most prayer time you are speaking with God asking for spiritual wisdom and spiritual guidance for earthly matters. It's spiritual communication that goes into heaven requesting that as it is in heaven, that it is on earth. Which is why the word says in 1 Thessalonians 5:17, "Pray without ceasing." You should always talk with God; it should be a regular habit that you have. Being that prayer is communication, never forget to allow God to speak to you. It's easy to make it a one-sided conversation, but in your silence, you can hear him speak, but you must listen, If you posture yourself as a student when you pray in times that you need to hear from God, you will be more open to listening rather than speaking.

Your prayer should be genuine and not religious, Jesus says in Matthew 6:5-8, "And when thou prayest, thou shalt not be as the hypocrites *are*: for they love to pray standing in the synagogues and in the corners of the streets, that they may be seen of men. Verily I say unto you, They have their reward.(6)But thou, when thou prayest, enter into thy closet, and when thou hast shut thy door, pray to thy Father which is in secret; and thy Father which seeth in secret shall reward thee openly.(7)But when ye pray, use not vain repetitions, as the heathen *do*: for they think that they shall be heard for their much speaking.(8)Be not ye therefore like unto them: for your Father knoweth what things ye have need of, before ye ask him." You must pray to God as if you are talking to your best friend but with the respect of him being your Father. Don't allow religion to form your words when you speak with him, allow your heart to speak. God is available all the time but are you willing to make time to really talk with him and hear from him. As stated in the bible, "Draw nigh to God, and he will draw nigh to you." James 3:8. You must make the effort to have a relationship, he's waiting on you.

Everything you read and should be applying has positioned your heart and mind to be centered around God. To be pure and driven to hold on to him and trust his every word. Everything if applied will allow you to have access to be heard when you pray to God. Do not be fooled, he is Holy and righteous and if you are in a righteous standing with him you don't have to worry about if he hears your prayers. The bible says, "The effectual fervent prayers of a righteous man availeth much." In James 5:16. Key word there is righteous, sin has the ability to stop your prayers from being answered, which is another trap the enemy sets to disconnect you from God. You will see victory if you simply apply the word of God to your life. You will be able to ask what you will and see it done in Jesus' name. Prayer is powerful, as a final bible study, here's a testimony about a widow who's son died and Elijah prayed to God.

"And the word of the LORD came unto him, saying,(9)Arise, get thee to Zarephath, which *belongeth* to Zidon, and dwell there: behold, I have commanded a widow woman there to sustain thee.(10)So he arose and went to Zarephath. And when he came to the gate of the city, behold, the widow woman *was* there gathering of sticks: and he called to her, and said, Fetch me, I pray thee, a little water in a vessel, that I may drink.(11)And as she was going to fetch *it*, he called to her, and said, Bring me, I pray thee, a morsel of bread in thine hand. (12)And she said, *As* the LORD thy God liveth, I have not a cake, but an handful of meal in a barrel, and a little oil in a cruse: and, behold, I *am* gathering two sticks, that I may go in and dress it for me and my son, that we may eat it, and die.(13)And Elijah said unto her, Fear not; go *and* do as thou hast said: but make me thereof a little cake first, and bring *it* unto me, and after make for thee and for thy son.(14)For thus saith the LORD God of Israel, The barrel of meal shall not waste, neither shall the cruse of oil fail, until the day *that* the LORD sendeth rain upon the earth.(15)And she went and did according to the saying of Elijah: and she, and he, and her house, did eat *many* days.(16)*And* the barrel of meal wasted not, neither did the cruse of oil fail, according to the word of the LORD, which he spake by Elijah.(17)And it came to pass after these things, *that* the son of the woman, the mistress of the house, fell sick; and his sickness was so sore, that there was no breath left in him.(18)And she said unto Elijah, What have I to do with thee, O thou man of God? art thou come unto me to call my sin to remembrance, and to slay my son?(19)And he said unto her, Give me thy son. And he took him out of her bosom, and carried him up into a loft, where he abode, and laid him upon his own bed.(20)And he cried unto the LORD, and said, O LORD my God, hast thou also brought evil upon the widow with whom I sojourn, by slaying her son?(21)And he stretched himself upon the child three times, and cried unto the LORD, and said, O LORD my God, I pray thee, let this child's soul come into him again.(22)And the LORD heard the voice of Elijah; and the soul of the child came into him again, and he revived.(23)And Elijah took the child, and brought him down out of the chamber into the house, and delivered him unto his mother: and Elijah said, See, thy son liveth.(24) And the woman said to Elijah, Now by this I know that thou art a man of God, and that the word of the Lord in thy mouth is truth.

Here is a woman who only has her son, and they are in the midst of a famine and Elijah tells her to give him her last. The very last meal that she said she was making for her and her son to die. Elijah went in his obedience to God, so he had no fear in telling her to trust him, because he was there because God sent him there. She obeyed and her and her house was able to eat for many days, but later on her son became sick and died. Elijah took her son into the upper room where he was staying and placed the boy on the bed and begin to pray to God. The bible says he cried unto the Lord and God heard the voice of Elijah and the child's life was restored. How amazing is that testimony! Not only did God fulfill and save them from dying the first time when she lost hope but even when sickness came to their house, God proved himself to be powerful through his servant's prayer. Prayer has the power to do anything if you are righteous and if you believe. Your prayers can achieve so many things in this earth, so if you are not praying as you should, consider this- You may be holding up your breakthrough to the next level, you may be holding someone's healing up…. all because you won't pray fervently and in righteousness.

God wants to partner with you, will you make him a priority and sacrifice sleep, events, tv, gym time, or simple be intentional about your time so that he can work through you. Because although he knows everything and truly doesn't need us to get his work done, he chooses to allow us to willingly take part in his miracles. Are you ready to be his living vessel?

Prayer

Father, forgive me for not putting you first.

Open my understanding and mind so that I

appreciate the time you have given me to spend

with you. Take me deeper into your word and

establish a stronger and better relationship with

me. Help me to prioritize things according to its

importance, which includes putting you first and

seeking you always. In Jesus name I ask these

things.

Amen.

Scripture(s) For Encouragement

"Be careful for nothing; but in every thing by prayer and supplication with thanksgiving let your request be made known unto God." Philippians 4:6

"Therefore I say unto you, What things soever ye desire, when ye pray, believe that ye receive them, and ye shall have them." Mark 11:24

"Call unto me, and I will answer thee, and shew thee great and mighty things, which thou knowest not."Jeremiah 33:3

"Our Father which art in heaven, Hallowed be thy

name.Thy kingdom come. Thy will be done in earth, as it is in heaven.Give us this day our daily bread.And forgive us our debts, as we forgive our debtors.And lead us not unto temptation, but deliver us from evil:For thine is the kingdom, and the power, and the glory,for ever.Amen"

Matthew 6:9-13

Closing

God wants to save you and restore you, so in return your relationship with him is restored. Just like he did for the widow woman and her son when she had lost hope and, on her way, to make their last meal, he sent Elijah to save them from dying. Well, God has sent Jesus to save you too over 2,000 years ago but you seem to have lost the fire you had for him in the very beginning, or you simply have been living a religious life and God desires to have a deeper relationship with you. However, life has tried to overwhelm you and somewhere down the line you lost your connection and/ or you're looking to connect with God. But just when you started to lose all hope and feeling like you can't hear him, nor see him in the dark hour, God assigned this book to restore you and remind you of the father that's ready and willing to cover you, if you allow him. This is your moment to choose to commit or recommit your life to Christ. To accept him as your personal savior and repent from all your sins and walk in the new man or woman of God. In addition, if you have not been baptized by water, you must be baptized by water and by the Holy Ghost.

Final Note from Author

As you come to the end of this book, I pray that you are closing this book with a deeper understanding and appreciation for the sacrifice of Jesus Christ and have accepted him as your personal savior. That you have repented from the sins that disconnect you from God and walk victoriously forward and upward. That you are fully aware of the tactics of the enemy, Satan, and how to combat his attacks. I pray that you embrace and walk in the commandment of love, and I pray that God fills you with his love, so that your walk will be fulfilled in all your gifts. Remember to stay connected to God, don't just say he's first but be diligent about making God first. Invite him in every decision concerning everything, don't make him an afterthought after you've moved. Allow him to guide you so that your path will be great and full of the promises and rewards he has for you while on this earth. Don't forget to be about his business by spreading love and being the example of holiness and righteousness. We as believers must take back our rightful place in being the head and not the tail in this world. We must allow people to see that there's hope and freedom when living a life for God. You will be in my prayers daily; may God continuously bless you with strength and understanding and prosperity.

-Troyal Tillman